DEVELOPING HIGH DELIVERY TEAMS

DEVELOPING HIGH DELIVERY TEAMS
A PRACTICAL HANDBOOK FOR LEADERS

REBECCA WATSON

AuthorHouse™
1663 Liberty Drive
Bloomington, IN 47403
www.authorhouse.com
Phone: 1-800-839-8640

© 2013 by Rebecca Watson. All rights reserved.

No part of this book may be reproduced, stored in a retrieval system, or transmitted by any means without the written permission of the author.

Published by AuthorHouse   12/18/2012

ISBN: 978-1-4772-5027-3 (sc)
ISBN: 978-1-4772-5028-0 (e)

Any people depicted in stock imagery provided by Thinkstock are models, and such images are being used for illustrative purposes only.
Certain stock imagery © Thinkstock.

This book is printed on acid-free paper.

Because of the dynamic nature of the Internet, any web addresses or links contained in this book may have changed since publication and may no longer be valid. The views expressed in this work are solely those of the author and do not necessarily reflect the views of the publisher, and the publisher hereby disclaims any responsibility for them.

Contents

Index	Page
Introduction	vii
Finding The Time	ix
Chapter 1—Team Bus	1
Chapter 2—The Vision	4
Chapter 3—SMART Goals	9
Chapter 4—The Strategy and Plan	15
Chapter 5—Roles	20
Chapter 6—Elephant in The Bus	25
Chapter 7—Team Meetings—How Teams Communicate	29
Chapter 8—Team Relationships	39
Chapter 9—External Barriers	47
Chapter 10—The Leader	50
Chapter 11—Managing Energy	57
Chapter 12—Celebrating Success	62
Acknowledgments	65

Introduction

Hello—I am Rebecca Watson owner of Brompton Associates.

My passion for helping people really enjoy their work came when I was a young commercial lawyer. I constantly felt as if someone was going to find me out! I was bored, yet anxious about the work and as it was really not the right career path for me, I was often unhappy, getting completely drunk on a Friday night, only to spend all of Sunday dreading Monday morning.

I realized that leadership and working in good teams could mean that people not only delivered a lot more collectively, but also really enjoyed coming to work. Luckily I went onto find my niche as a specialist Corporate Coach and now feel that it is my path to help guide leaders of people to gain results and become the popular leader that everyone wants to work with.

Since starting to coach Executives in 2001, I have worked with 100s of leaders around the world. I have experienced many forms of 'Team Coaching' that include teams playing games together and team coaches psychoanalyzing all the team members and reporting back.

What I didn't see much of is **HOW** you get a team to improve performance.

Managing to get a team of people to deliver for an organisation, whether that be a small business or a large global corporate is a tricky thing to do! The science behind group dynamics and collaborative entrepreneurship is continuously being evolved. The ability to Coach a Team whether that be the England football team, or a project management team within a bank is being studied in more depth. The successful strategies are becoming clearer.

In this book I have set out simple diagrams to help explain a topic that is complex and can become highly theoretical and academic.

Rebecca Watson

This book is the product of many years experience and research in Executive and Team Coaching. It is not a one size fits all guide, but a programme of exercises that can be carried out with a team over time that have been tried and tested in reality. It's these exercises that I'm going to share with you so that you can run them with your own team and see the results immediately.

Finding The Time

Do you feel as if you are working really hard and long hours but not really achieving results as quickly as you expected? Are there more strategic things that your team 'should' do but never have time because you are doing the 'day to day' stuff?

This is normally the first problem that the leaders I coach face—they know they need to do something different but they don't have time to do it, or even think about it.

SO

- stop being the hamster on a wheel
- get off for a few minutes—the world won't end, the company won't collapse
- breathe and allow your head to settle
- start to think strategically and you'll go to the next level of leadership

I used to send leaders my 6 month Team Coaching Programme which entailed me working with the team for 6 days (one day a month over 6 months). The leader would be really keen to start with and book a day or two, then the third day would get moved, I would need to chase for commitment and the leader and team would say 'I really want to work with you, the team found it so valuable and I can see changes already but . . . .' They would allow all the 'urgent' day-to-day stuff to crowd in. (They couldn't stay off the hamster wheel long enough to completely get rid of it and become their own masters).

Look after your time (it's the most valuable commodity), if you're going to really change the way you and your team work then commit the time and keep that protected for your team. The highest business priority is enabling your team to produce more.

Benefits from Team Coaching

- Increased Team delivery
- Board Level Teams—increase company revenue, saleability and reputation as a good employer in the market
- Increased Team Morale—everyone should feel happier and more excited about their work contribution
- Embedded Learning—new ways of working gets modeled down into all other teams below this team in the organizational structure
- Cultural Change—the effects of a team implementing these strategies will extend far beyond just that one team, the ripple effect outwards and downwards will make the work practices of all those that interact with this team more effective
- Leadership in the team will improve providing a much better model for others to aspire to
- By reading, understanding and trying out the exercises in this book, you are training yourself in how to create high delivery teams, how to coach your own team and how to run effective meetings
- The fall out—those that are not a good fit for the organization culturally, often voluntarily leave. Those that are in the wrong role can move to another role within the organization and the organization gains higher productivity from that resource

Quick Audit for CEOs

1) How much of my week is spent with my Executive Team? (go to Finding The Time and Chapter 7)

2) When I think of my team, are there members who I feel aren't engaged, aren't good enough, aren't focused 100% on growing this organisation? (go to Chapter 1, Chapter 5, Chapter 10, Chapter 11)

Developing High Delivery Teams

3) What do the Executive Team picture when they think of the company's vision and what the company will be doing differently in the future? Is this aligned? (go to Chapter 2)

4) What are the Organisations top 3 goals? Are they just monetary goals, or do they relate to activities that people understand? Do we have a way of measuring where we are now with these goals and a way to measure when we have reached them? (go to Chapter 3)

5) Do we have a clear plan that is accessible by each member of the Executive Team? (go to Chapter 4)

6) Does each member of my team know what their department is expected to deliver against the plan? Do they have a way of measuring where they are against the plan? (go to Chapter 5)

7) In my Executive Team meetings, do I get all the measurements reported to me that I need in order to understand how the organisation is tracking against the plan? (go to Chapter 7)

8) Does everyone in the team respect and listen to each other? Who are the people who don't get on? How is this dynamic replicated throughout entire departments within the organisation? How does this prevent the organisation from growing? (go to Chapter 7)

9) What do I really think about my team members? Are there any negative thoughts in there? How does this affect the energy in the team? (go to Chapter 10 and Chapter 11)

10) What do I really think about the market, the organisation, my ability to lead it through these current times? Are there any negative thoughts in there? How does this affect my personal energy and the impression I'm sending out to the world? Am I able to turn this around to attract success to me? (go to Chapter 11)

Chapters 1 - 12

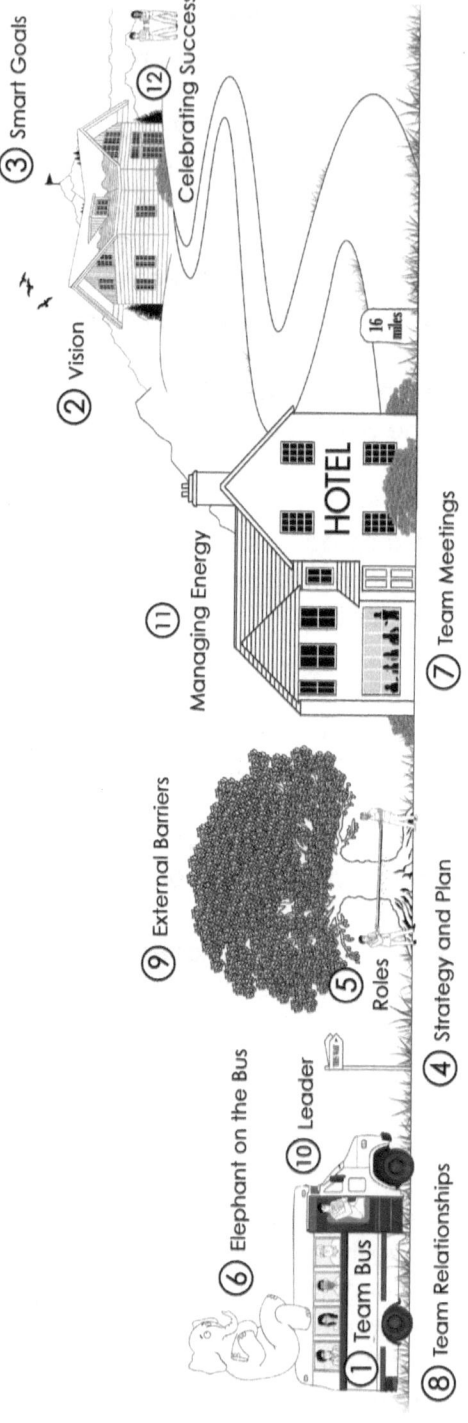

I wanted to create a memorable diagram to explain the Team Coaching work I did. So I came up with this fun cartoon image. Each section of the image relates to a chapter in this book.

You might find that you already have a clear, shared vision, but the team is being held back by a poor working relationship between two or three members. The only chapters that need to be completed in chapter correct order, are chapters 1-4. The other chapters you can dip in and out of as you see fit.

Often restructures occur so that team members can be removed. The Leader restructures as a quick and easy way to get rid of team members simply based on their inability to get on with other team members, agree with the team leader, or get their work done. This may not have anything to do with their capability (i.e. their skill set) they may well be capable but other factors that come into play stop them from performing (see Chapter 5).

We want to ensure that we have the right people on the bus from the start however sometimes we are unaware of how skilful someone is because they do not feel able to demonstrate their skills fully. Throughout the development of a team, hopefully these skills come to the fore, and the team's ability and motivation to learn new skills is also increased.

Chapter 1—Team Bus

Do you Have a Team?

The definition of a team is a group of people who need to work together to deliver an outcome. Often a manager has a group of people who report to them and they have regular 'team' meetings, however the group of people are not actually a team, there may be two or more teams within this group of people.

- So are your team all working towards a common goal?
- Do you have a team of 2 working together and a team of 4 working towards a totally separate business goal?
- Do you get natural groupings of people in team meetings?

(One of the key indicators that a manager has a group of people reporting to them that are not actually a team, but the manager doesn't realise and continues to have 'team' meetings, is that the people in that team will naturally communicate with those they need to in order to get the job done. There will be a natural divide within the group that is not based on personalities, but based on commercial reality.)

Example

I was asked to facilitate a team meeting at a global bank in London, the team were not communicating well and the manager wanted to focus on this in our meeting. There were only 7 people in the team, however even as I entered the room, I could sense that there were alliances within the team. Two of the women sat at the end of the table having a laugh like old friends and the rest of the team sat slightly removed from them around the table.

The manager felt that their team was slightly dysfunctional because although the two women communicated between themselves very well, they didn't share much with the rest of the team, or even seem interested in what the others were doing. This frustrated him hugely as he felt it was a reflection on his ability to manage well.

I asked the team what they did and two distinct areas of work emerged. The two women were responsible for a wider reaching regulatory and compliance part of the work and the rest of the team were directly involved in operational work. I asked each person in the team who they most needed to speak to during the day to get their work done and it became obvious that there were two teams here that simply reported to the same person. There was little business impact if the two teams did not communicate, so to save time, they didn't!

Once this became obvious, the manager suddenly laughed, 'so you mean that I've brought you in to help us all communicate more and what you've done is explain why it's better use of time for us not to really communicate?' I replied 'yes, actually people will naturally communicate with those they need to (unless they feel uncomfortable with that person), to get their work done'.

He went away, realising that he now needed to run two separate team meetings, and perhaps bring other staff into some of these meetings too, as there were virtual teams forming for different projects. He also realised that his management style was just fine, he didn't have to have everyone communicating to the same level within his direct reports as there were two teams, not one.

Exercise 1

- Ask the team to write down their individual answer to 'what is it you are aiming to do for this organisation?'
- Share the answers and place all answers on a whiteboard.
- See if there is a consensus of a team goal or maybe several team goals.

- Name each goal on the whiteboard with a circle around it. Ask team members to place their name in the circle(s) that represent the goals that they feel most aligned to when they come to work each day.
- See where the spread of names lie—if there are a group of people per goal, then this indicates that there may be teams within a larger team. If the names are spread fairly evenly across all the different circles, then it indicates that you have one team with a group of goals. Note there may be sub-teams with an overall higher-level goal that all members link into.

Chapter 2—The Vision

Where is the Team Bus Heading?

Useful Distinctions:

A vision—in its pure form is an imagined picture of what the world will look like when we reach our goals.

Mission Statement—is a verbal statement to describe the vision or goals.

Joint Vision = Motivated Team

For a team of people to feel motivated, they need to be able to see the end goal. To visualise what it will be like to have already delivered their goals (whether that goal has an actual physical output like building a block of flats, or is more esoteric, like improving the way we interact with our customers).

Once each person in the team has 'time travelled' into the imaginary future and experienced in their own imagination what it would feel like to be part of the team that has achieved this goal, then each team member will create their own motivation to gain this goal.

Example

We are all motivated by different things so e.g. Tim, Sam and Alex are a team of project managers working to complete a block of flats. When they are guided by their team leader to do the Visualisation Exercise, Tim feels a sense of personal achievement because the block of flats looks so cool and modern, he can hear his friends admiring comments when they drive past and he tells them he helped build it. Sam visualises the three of them going for drinks at the end of the project and laughing in the pub. He feels a sense of camaraderie and is motivated by not letting his mates down. Alex's picture is less clear but he has an inner sense of personally developing his skills and moving towards greater personal career goals.

The Purpose of the Exercise

The purpose of the Exercise is to illicit motivation in each team member and for each team member to get a clear picture of the end deliverable (easier if it is a physical output but still possible if less tangible). The vision needs to be one that is appealing to each team member, if it is not then they will want to 'get off the bus and join another one going somewhere else!' This can happen and people leave the team, which is not a bad outcome if they aren't committed to the team vision.

Don't Get Analysis Paralysis

Beware of the common problem for teams just doing visioning and never getting on with action. Make sure that the Vision is not 10 years away so that the, Goals and Plan are stuck to for long enough for the team to actually deliver something!

- How rapidly is your organisation changing?
- If your team set a 3 year goal, is it likely to reach it?
- How long can the team keep focused on a goal? Is 3 or 6 months a more realistic timeframe?

Bland and Confusing Vision/Mission Statements

Often leaders will have a paragraph of written words to describe their vision. These words are often high level business speak with a few comparative terms like 'the best' or 'the biggest' etc. When each person in the company reads this 'statement of a vision' they will make a different picture in their minds eye. So a company of 1000 people will have 1000 different pictures that represent their vision.

No one is aligned and the vision is confusing, conflicting or simply not inspiring to most. The vision MUST be a picture because by definition it is visual. The words must describe the equivalent of being in the Chalet (see main diagram page xii), what you will see, feel and hear when you have made it to the Chalet in the mountains. It must be inspiring enough for people to want to make the effort to get there, otherwise they'll just not be motivated. It must be realistic, so they believe it's possible, in their lifetime!

Exercise 2—Obtaining a Team Vision

- **Where?** If possible hold a meeting for the whole team over a longer period than just a team meeting (3hrs is good time) in a meeting room that is as high up in your office building as possible with large windows that are easy to see out of (this helps to create in our brains, the ability to start visioning, and seeing into the distance in space and in time).
- **Getting the Right Vibe** Start with a little game to connect everyone to the part of their brain that is creative and visually orientated. The game is for each person to take it in turns

to describe to the group the most beautiful place they have ever been. They need to 'paint a picture' of this place in everyone's mind's eye. The group then ask questions of the describer about this place. The questions can be clarifying what the place looks like, how it feels, what sounds you can hear, where are you seeing this place from (i.e. are you in the picture looking out through your own eyes, or are you viewing it from a distance).

- **What is the Timeframe for the Vision?** Next we need to get a consensus of time frame for the vision—is it 6 months or 3yrs? To do this ask each person to decide what timeframe is workable in your culture (some cultures change so rapidly that a 3 month vision and set of goals feels manageable) and everyone should be able to come up with a timeframe that 'feels right' and 'feels realistic'. Note it is possible to have a short term and a long term vision but you do need a consensus of opinion so everyone is working to the same timeframe.
- **Visioning/Daydreaming**. Now you need to allocate time for each person to daydream and close their eyes, or look out of the window and imagine how it will be when they reach their destination in the timeframe that has been set. Ask what is possible in 6 months time? What will your workplace look like? What will you have achieved? What will people be saying about this team? How will you feel when you walk into work and go through your day? Then let everyone's imagination run wild—(this time should be silent in the room and last a good 10 minutes).
- Next you need to collate the thoughts and feelings that everyone has come up with on the whiteboard. This is the first part of forming a collective vision. It is important for each person to contribute here, and for all contributions to be welcome, however they are stated (e.g. some people will state how they feel/don't feel, what they hear/don't hear others saying, what they are saying/not saying to themselves, what they see/don't see anymore. So long as everyone has their own representation of the vision and that it is possible for them to realise this through the goals

(Chapter 3) that are set by the team, it doesn't matter that they differ).
- Once all the thoughts and pictures are recorded on the whiteboard, let the team discuss their ideas and ask questions of each other to ensure that they can understand the pictures that are in each other's mind (this is obviously impossible in reality, but it is the nearest we can get through language, to a collective vision).
- A clearer picture of the team vision should be forming. People may be arguing over what is important, and achievable so note these disparities but let the team agree on a realistic vision in the timeframe (it is possible to put other visions on the diagram that the team feel are achievable in a longer time period (the mountain beyond the first mountain).

Chapter 3—SMART Goals

SMART is the common acronym developed originally by Paul Meyer and although many teams that I've worked with don't like the disciplined thinking that is required for creating SMART Goals, it still seems to be one of the key characteristics of a high performing team.

    S—Specific
    M—Measurable
    A—Achievable
    R—Relevant
    T—Time bound

Setting Key Goals

Once the vision has been 'experienced' by everyone and discussed, then some Key Goals can be set up.

Sometimes the Vision is of the end Goal, but sometimes a Vision is wider reaching and enticing and the team's role is to achieve one or two key goals that will contribute towards the vision.

Example

I worked with a team of IT managers within a global bank. Part of their vision was to be seen as an integral part of the overall IT services to the bank. (The team was originally a poor relation within the overall IT department because it has been used as a dumping ground for all sorts of different applications that were not valued as important to the bank.)

Once the team had a vision of the future, which included feeling that their work was valued and important as well as adding value to their internal customers, they felt motivated to work together and turn things around. Out of the vision came the start of forming several goals;

- one was to improve the usability of a specific IT application,
- a second goal, however was to be seen as useful and integral to the overall IT service by their peers.

These two goals had separate outcomes and paths to achieving them. Each was set up as a project in its own right. They decided on a timeframe of a year to achieve the overall vision and some of the goals were going to be achieved within a shorter timeframe.

SMART Goals

Most management training courses will have covered setting SMART goals, so I don't intend to do that here.

Measuring your Team

The measurement part of the Goal is often the part that is missing. In my opinion it is the single biggest factor of successful or unsuccessful teams in the workplace.

- What are your current team goals?
- How will you know that you have reached them?
- Do you know where the team is currently with regard to reaching these goals?

Note: The measurements of a Goal don't always have to be objective, they can often be subjective measurements within the team e.g. the team currently rate themselves as a 2/10 for communicating to each other and knowing specific actions that they are going to take to increase that, the team can re-rate themselves subjectively again in 3 months or whenever the goal is to be reached.

Example

A customer services team wanted to improve the ways it dealt with customers that they really couldn't help because the customer was complaining about something out of the company's control.

The first thing I asked was 'how do you currently deal with these types of customers?' I then asked 'how do you know what your customers feel about this right now?'

The team didn't have a way of measuring customer satisfaction for these types of customers so what we needed to do was a survey of some sort that measured the current state of the relationships that they had with these customers.

Once this survey had been carried out, it was possible to conduct the same survey to ensure that they had reached their goal. To make it specific they asked the customers to rate the service from 1-10. That meant that they could measure where they currently were with their customers, then after following their plan to enhance customer service to this group they could do the survey again and see if they had reached their target of 8 out of 10 as an average rating. Once they put a deadline to the work, this became a SMART Goal.

Exercise 3a—Setting SMART Goals

- **Setting the Goals.** Once the Vision is formed and understood by everyone, the next step is to set out the Goals. (Note: In order for everyone in the team to realise their vision, there may be more than just Business Goals e.g. a goal may be about how the team works together rather than what it will deliver). Teams that need to create their own Goals (normally the executive board/ business owners) will need additional time here to brainstorm ideas. Allocate a large part of the agenda to brainstorming, this allows people to relax as they feel they have enough time to play with ideas that may not necessarily lead to an outcome. Welcome ALL ideas, however ridiculous they appear and write each one on a whiteboard—or stickers around the room. In a team of more than 6 people it may be worth splitting into smaller groups of 3 to 4 and then collating the ideas. The element of 'play' and 'having fun' needs to be in the room, so enjoy this part, have a laugh, the vibe wants to be flexible, let people sit where they want, walk around, get a drink, look out of the window for long periods of time. This all facilitates creativity.

- **What if the Team gets Blocked?** If you reach a block, where ideas have dried up its important to spend 5-10 minutes playing some sort of game that allows the energy of the group to become more fluid and to get everyone connecting the left and right sides of the brain (this needs to happen for creativity to flow) Many ice-breaker type games can be found on the internet.
- Once the Goals have been agreed—and checked against SMART Goal criteria they need to be recorded on a flipchart. I often draw a rough sketch of the diagram on page xii and write the SMART goals on the right hand side of the mountain.
- **Setting Measurements of Success.** Once the Goals are also recorded then the team can brainstorm how they will measure whether or not they have reached each Goal. The question to ask is 'How will we know we've got there?' These measurements also need to be recorded, so everything is in writing and can be referred back to at a later date.

Exercise 3b to Test SMART Goals:

Note: To test if a goal is SMART, one option is to have someone outside of the team/organisation read the goal that has been set up and ask basic questions about the goal, so that they can describe to themselves exactly what that goal means and how they will know that it has been reached (i.e. the Measurement part of SMART) Alternatively the team must ask themselves some key questions set out below:

- Firstly question every statement in the goal with 'What Specifically?' 'How many?' 'Who specifically?' 'When specifically?' (see Case Study below)
- Secondly ask 'what will I see when this goal is reached?' (the deliverable may be a document, a diagram, a spreadsheet, a method/process/model or a physical output like a new computer network) Note: The purpose of some teams is to ultimately change the behaviour of others who work in the organisation e.g. If a team is responsible for implementing a new working process, then although they may write the process and communicate it, their real goal is to have their target audience following the process. The measurement of this goal then will be based on what the team will see and hear their target audience doing differently in the workplace due to their new process.
- Thirdly is the goal achievable? If the team don't all feel its possible to achieve the goal at all, or in the timeframe, then it becomes demotivating
- Fourthly how relevant will it be to the organisation if the team gets this goal? It needs to be a goal that is worth achieving, is tied into a larger purpose that ideally is linked to the organisations overall aims
- Lastly ensure that the time frame set, is one that will motivate, rather than create unnecessary stress, or cause team members to give up before they've started!

Case Study:

I worked with an entrepreneurial charity, which initiates and delivers practical solutions that help us to live within a fair share of the earth's resources.

In November 2010, they held a company away day. One of their key outcomes for the day was for all their employees to be able to visualise the goals that they needed to achieve by 2012. The executive management team also wanted everyone in the company to be motivated and excited by these goals, and know what they needed to do to contribute to achieving them within their teams.

I was facilitating the day and suggested that a fun way to represent their team goals for 2012 was for each team leader (there were 6 teams including the executive management team) to find magazine pictures, or draw diagrams to represent the goals that they needed to achieve by 2012.

Next we took a wallpaper sized roll of paper and cut it into 6 equal length pieces of around 4 meters long. During the day these 6 lines of paper were laid out on the floor. a line representing time was marked along the middle of the paper and one end represented the date of the away day, at the other end, the team leaders marked 2012 and at this end, they stuck their pictures and drew diagrams to demonstrate the goals that their team needed to achieve by this date.

The teams tested each goal to ensure that they were SMART e.g. one team's goal was initially worded 'to capitalise on past projects and influence other groups to set up similar projects'—the team asked 'What do we mean by 'capitalise'?'—they meant set up a case study with the key learnings and process used to set up an environmentally friendly wood burner. Next they asked 'what do we specifically mean by 'influence'?'—they meant to meet and persuade people to set up more environmentally friendly wood burners. Next they asked 'Which 'other groups'?'—they decided on three specific London councils that they would target and the specific people they knew, that worked for those councils and had the power to agree to set up environmentally friendly wood burners.

So the new SMART Goal was reworded to 'To write a case study setting out the key learnings and the process used to set up an environmentally friendly wood burner, to meet x, y and z from a, b and c Councils and persuade them to copy our process and set up at least one environmentally friendly wood burner each'.

This goal was specific, measureable, achievable and relevant, it was time-bound as the team needed to achieve it by a specific date in 2012.

Chapter 4—The Strategy and Plan

Which Route Will the Team Bus Take?

Once an enticing Vision and SMART Goals have been set up, the next phase of mobilising a team to deliver them.

The word 'strategy' often intimidates people who feel that 'doing strategy' is a highly skilled job that they may not have been trained for, however in reality (unless you are a specialist Strategist) the strategic part is simply deciding the best way to get to the end goals.

Example

If you were to travel from London to Paris, there are several different ways you could travel—you could go all the way by Eurostar, you could fly from several different airports in London, or you could drive to Dover and take your car on the Ferry. If you had plenty of time, but not much money you could hitchhike, or cycle! You chose your best option depending on an array of factors (cost, time, energy involved, what you would like to experience on the journey . . .) this then becomes your strategy. So generally in business the strategy for a team to reach their goals is often obvious and simple (depending on how political the environment in which you work is).

If the Strategy is the route you chose to take, then the Plan is the actual steps that you need to take to get there—the Plan will always be action orientated, specific and time-bound.

Case Study:

A small head hunting company wanted to differentiate itself from the competition in order to be more saleable in the future. They had a goal to sell the company in 5 years time for as much as they could at that time but set a minimum of £x million.

They met to discuss their strategy and brainstormed ideas of what they could do differently—some of the ideas they came up with were—expanding into different markets, specialising in the Media and Technology field, acquiring a competitor to become the biggest in their market sector etc . . . One of the ideas was to set up a services side to the business that provided executive coaching, highly targeted training workshops and HR consultancy to their existing client base (which comprised of many CEOs and Executives of small to medium-sized companies in Europe). They decided to go with this as their strategy.

Next they needed a plan and some key milestones. They appointed one of the partners to build the new services arm of the business. This partner began by setting up a low cost coaching programme for Executives and marketed it to their existing customers. This was to test the market before proceeding with the rest of the plan, which included hiring suitable experts who could deliver the services they were offering and a business development manager.

The new team met to set a plan of actions that needed to be taken for the business to build. Key milestones were set so that the team could measure their progress as well as celebrate getting from one point to the next (this helped the team to focus on the short term and stay motivated—sometimes a plan of several years seems too overwhelming and actually de-motivates people).

Part of the plan involved meeting again to re-assess the plan every 6 months to ensure that they could respond to the market and adapt the plan to provide what the market was wanting, rather than stick rigidly to a plan that may not deliver the end goal (building a service business for senior Executives)

Exercise 4a: Creating the Team Strategy

- Once you have the diagram with the Vision, Goals and Measurements, it is possible to set up milestones on the journey towards the Vision. These Milestones are like smaller Goals and should also pass the SMART test.

The team must brainstorm what they feel will be obvious milestones e.g. Key projects completed within a programme of works. These milestones need to be placed in time along the route.

- You may find that at the same time as brainstorming the milestones, someone (the critic, see Chapter 6) will also see some of the potential potholes/barriers and these need to be welcomed and recorded on the diagram too.
- At this point, we want the team to be creative, and come up with alternative routes to their goal (alternative strategies)—it is possible to add alternative routes around potholes, and end up with a fairly messy looking diagram, but it is the quality of the thinking that will be important. Again this needs to be a fun exercise, rather than the team getting bogged down with possible potholes/barriers. Simply mark all the potholes/barriers with no need to find solutions at this stage.
- One of the milestones may also include reviewing the vision, goals, measurements or strategy and plan. (Note: some teams review the vision and goals so regularly that they never actually deliver anything. This is a danger for teams where the leader is afraid of failing. Their fear of delivering something that is not right, is greater than their fear of not delivering anything, so procrastination and/or almost constant re-working of the plan occurs. If this has been happening in a team, the team will not have delivered anything concrete for some time, and there will be a high degree of frustration or complete disengagement from team members).
- Eventually the team needs to be brought out of the creative/discussion stage and settle on an agreed route (strategy). It may be possible to have route a, but if a perceived pothole/barrier occurs then switch to route b. Or it may be more suitable for the team to decide that they will start with route a, and reassess their strategy regularly (in which case these reassessment meetings need to be embedded in the plan and this is a strategy in itself).

- An agreed strategy should be recorded (a Strategic Plan document).

Creating the Plan

The exercise I use for creating The Plan is a way of getting the team to buy in to the plan and creating a clear pathway towards the team goal that is visual (often people get bogged down reading strategy documents, when what they want is to see a clear pathway towards their goals.

The representation of a Plan visually means that everyone can see where they are going (literally) this helps teams manage anxiety around whether they will achieve their goals. It also helps the team measure their success (or if they are falling behind in the plan).

Milestones

A longer term Goal can also be too daunting and then the team loses motivation when they think of everything they have to do. With the creation of milestones, it allows teams to focus on immediate actions to get to the next milestone, which is more motivating as it is more immediately achievable.

Exercise 4b: Creating the Team Plan

- Hold a team meeting in a room with a large whiteboard. Draw a line from left to right across the whiteboard, which represents time (we tend to represent time in space with the future to our right and the past to our left).
- Clearly set out the end goals on the right hand side of the diagram with the measurements listed too (see Chapter 3).
- There needs to be clearly marked measurements of time along the timeline too, so that the detail can be filled in month by month. The team need to be able to recreate a movie image in their heads of the future and what they will be doing to achieve the milestones and eventually the end goals.

- This exercise will be very difficult if they milestones and goals are not SMART, it will highlight the need to revisit the milestones and goals if the team cannot agree what needs to be done to reach them. Every action should be marked on the line with a deadline, the plan should be populated with little explanations of the actions that the team will need to take. Everything marked on the plan should be an action (using simple verbs such as 'draft', 'design', 'model', 'persuade', 'inform', 'send', 'receive'.

Chapter 5—Roles

Who does What?

How to Energise the Team

As a team it is useful to discuss who can achieve each action on the Plan, this not only means that each team member is held accountable for delivering their part of the plan, but from a performance management point of view, the team manager can track how each team member is doing.

- What specific pieces of work do each of your team members enjoy?
- What do they dislike doing?
- Does anything in the list of 'dislikes' match with another team members' list of 'enjoy'?

In a high performing team each member will be doing what they love doing, and will be able to pass on what they don't like doing to another team member who loves that. In this way all members are working to maximum performance, motivation and enjoyment.

Like a team of formula 1 mechanics, each has a role to play. In this way the team manager also gets the best person to do each job—strong teams are all different, but appreciate each other's differences.

It is key that each member of the team can openly and honestly talk about the type of actions that they love to do and that energise them as well as the type of activities that they don't like and that they put off, or do and then feel tired, irritable or anxious.

Obviously there are jobs that no-one in the team likes to do, and perhaps this is the time to hire someone who likes doing these jobs, or more realistically support each other to do these jobs and celebrate when they are done.

Am I Lazy or Just Not Motivated?

Note: One of our key failings as leaders is to assume that if someone isn't motivated, then they are lazy, however that lazy person in your team will be highly motivated to do something else like packing and getting up early to catch a flight for their holiday! I believe people are not innately 'lazy' they are just in the wrong job. If they could trust a manager to not judge them, but help them find a role that they felt good at and interested in, then they wouldn't cling to a job they disliked and organisations would not be carrying so much inefficiency in their workforce.

Skills Gaps?

Once a team starts to develop a detailed plan, it becomes clear that perhaps not all the skills required to deliver the plan are held in the team—this allows the team manager to determine training needs for existing team members or the need to hire new skills into the team.

Training Plans

A training plan cannot be written without the team first covering the steps in chapters 1—4. Without knowing what the team needs to deliver, by when and how, it is impossible to know where the gaps in skills lie.

With a training plan you will be able to coach the team member who is struggling to deliver because they are in the process of building their skill set and experience in this area. You will also be able to build a case for replacement if a team member is unable to deliver the actions that the team requires them to deliver.

Example:

A team of IT consultants were mostly working on client sites in London, however they were also responsible for generating new business. They hated making phone calls to prospective clients and this was a specialist job that required someone with their knowledge to do, so there was no option of hiring someone else to do it.

The manager decided that the best time to speak to people about possible new work would be Friday afternoons, so the whole team blocked off this time in their calendars and came into the open plan office to make their calls:

1) They began by spending 30 minutes listing the clients that they would call.

2) Next they had a 10 minute break. In this time, they used some coaching exercises to build confidence and relax them before they made their calls.

3) For the next 60 minutes they all made their calls.

4) They then had another break and celebrated any possible leads that they had generated. This allowed team camaraderie to build and for members to support each other.

5) The last 60 minutes was again spent cold calling.

6) When that hour was up, they left the office as a team to go to the nearest pub and celebrate a challenging job having been completed.

After a few weeks, one of the consultants actually told me that he now looked forward to Friday afternoons, because although he still didn't like cold calling, for him, he had come to view the afternoons as more of a team building activity and chance to have a laugh with his colleagues!

Exercise 5: Developing Clearly Marked Roles and Personal Development Plans—For the Team Leader Only

- The Leader is to give each team member a copy of the plan—either in hardcopy or on screen (if its in the form of a MS Project Gantt Chart) and to ask each team member a) what parts of the plan would you like to do and feel you have the experience and skills? b) What part of the plan would you not like to do but feel you might end up doing because you have the experience and the skills? c) Is there a part of the plan that you'd you like to do but feel you would need support to gain the experience and skills and what type of support would you need?
- The Leader then marks out along the plan in another colour who they think would be best at doing each action—obviously some actions may need more than one team member. This will also highlight any team members that the Leader doesn't have any faith in and therefore an area for intense coaching/training, or an honest conversation about what they can do.
- Next the Leader compares their innate choice of who does what with the responses from their questions a)—c) to each team member. Here is the opportunity for the Leader to develop their team. The Leader may decide to swap some of the names over to enable the team to be happy with doing what they are best at (a), less of what they lose energy doing (b) and some of what they'd like to develop (c).
- The Leader may also at this point decide to bring in new skills (if this is possible) or mentor individuals themselves if the Leader has the skill but no one else in the team does. The Leader can add to team members' Personal Development Plans—sighting the action to be completed on the plan, the experience/skill required and how it will be gained (mentoring from the Leader or another person in the team/organisation, coaching or training).
- Next the Leader must have a 1:1 conversation with each team member and agree the actions that they will be responsible for (and those that they will not in some cases).

- Once everyone in the team is happy with their own role within the team plan, the Leader can hold a team meeting to run through the plan and actions again, sighting who will do what and ensure that there are clear boundaries between roles.
- During this meeting step the team through each section of the plan in time and each team member telling the group what they will be doing at each action point and then when they will hand over to the next team member along the line. Ensure each team member talks through what they think they will be doing at each action point and what it is they will have achieved before they hand over to the next team member on the plan.

Chapter 6—Elephant in The Bus

Honest Open Communication

Often teams have a vision, a sound strategy and plan, clear roles, however communication is not honest and open. This is the barrier then to the team maximising their potential.

As in all good relationships, communication is key.

- What can't the Team talk about?
- Is there an obvious topic or topics that the team feel is unsafe to discuss?
- Have the team tried to talk about these things but in doing so experienced high emotions from team members (either angry, upset, embarrassed or simply storming out)?
- Is there something that is so obvious to everyone in the team but one member (potentially the leader)?

One of the key roles of an external professional Team Coach is to work with a team to the point where each member feels 'safe' enough to say what they'd really like to say. They may chose at first to speak directly to me and I would ultimately encourage them to voice this within the group if it's a team matter (as opposed to a one to one relationship with someone).

How you get an Elephant in The Bus

If teams have tried to discuss an emotive topic and failed to manage the emotions in the room, then they are building a negative memory of what happens when they try and resolve that particular issue and eventually they will tacitly agree not to go there.

If the Elephant Stays In The Bus

The danger of this is that the emotions that team members are feeling regarding this topic are still there. The problem is still there, and is likely to be reoccurring if not dealt with. The energy needed for humans to NOT say what they want and NOT show how they are feeling is wasted energy that could be used more productively. Eventually team members will feel unhappy working in this team. The team will gain a reputation of having a 'weird atmosphere' or being a 'boring' team to work in.

Dealing with Team Baggage

There are many different exercises to get the Elephant in The Bus out on the table so to speak, however in my experience, once a team has an Elephant in The Bus, then its hard for the team alone to solve it (because it's the dynamic within the members of the team that caused it in the first place). Sometimes the team members change and 'fresh energy' from someone new who isn't 'scared' to mention The Elephant, or doesn't even know its such a taboo subject will give the team a chance to discuss their past. The best exercise here, however is for the team Leader to bring in an external, independent facilitator /team coach who is experienced with group dynamics and creating safe environments for people to open up with how they feel. If the company has an experienced and trusted member of HR/Organisational Development who can facilitate the discussion then that is also advised, although often the issues are so contentious, or potentially destructive, that the team won't trust someone internal.

Exercise 6: Removing The Elephant (For Experienced Team Coach/ Facilitator/Mediator)

- The team Leader engages a Team Coach who they feel they can trust to deal with the team dynamics and unspoken emotions with care, compassion and non-judgement (its important that the external professional doesn't take sides

Developing High Delivery Teams

but simply asks of themselves 'what does this person need to move past this block right now?')
- The team Leader explain in advance to the team that they have set aside some time (a day/half day, perhaps off-site) to assist the team to work better together. (At this point, some team members have been known to not turn up, as they see this as their best strategy for 'keeping safe' around the issue that they fear will arise, but there is not really anything one can do about that, and if the a critical mass within the team shift their stance on the issue, then often this is enough to shake things up and help the team become 'less stuck').
- The day arrives and the Team Coach meets each team member privately to get their take on things and to help build a trusted confidence between them. (Its important that each team member knows that what they say privately to the Team Coach will be kept in the strictest of confidences and not reported back to anyone else in the team).
- Once each member has been met privately, the Team Coach will have a clearer picture of the history and emotions that some team members may still be holding.
- The team then meet together and the Team Coach will facilitate a 'light' exercise that doesn't mean the team are forced to discuss the Elephant straight away. This enables the Team Coach to observe the team dynamics and also allows the team to feel more relaxed with the Team Coach.
- During this process the Team Coach may decide to introduce the Elephant into the team discussion—they may not however, depending on how contentious the issue is, whether the issue is really a clash between two team members (in which case mediation between the two would be better than dragging the whole team into it) or if the issues are unwittingly caused by the Leader (in which case perhaps intense 1:1 Leadership Coaching may be more useful).
- Often Elephants in the room are caused by changes outside the team's control that the team feel threatened by (holding fear) or they feel the changes are unfair (holding anger). It

may even be a change that the team needs to mourn but has not had a forum in which to do this formally (holding sadness). Often people are unaware that they have been holding these emotions, or they feel they can't express them because they should always be positive. This misgiving causes no end of problems within organisations and once the Team Coach can help the team identify what they're holding and give them permission and a safe, confidential place to express them, then the Elephant slowly goes away . . .

Chapter 7—Team Meetings—How Teams Communicate

How teams communicate is one of the key ingredients to high performing teams. Members within teams may have ad hoc communication but the main forum for communication as a team is in team meetings. In my mind there are two areas that can change to help teams communicate more effectively and I have split them in this chapter for simplicity:

- Part 1—Team Meetings. One area I concentrate on in this chapter is for teams managing their team meeting better.
- Part 2—Group Dynamics. The second area is how the team actually communicate during the meeting.

Death By Meeting—The Boredom Test

Often organisations have too many meetings, people spend all day rushing from one meeting to the next and at 6pm they have to actually start doing the work generated by these meetings. This is usually because meetings are not run efficiently (with an agreed outcome from the start and a chairperson to keep everyone on topic). They are often automatically scheduled for an hour when really a solution to a problem might be found in 20minutes if everyone's mind was concentrated on just this one issue.

If you find yourself texting, checking emails or simply daydreaming because you are bored in a meeting, then either you are in the wrong job or there is no real need for you to be sitting through these conversations. Hopefully it's the latter and being bored is great feedback from the body, to tell you that you are not spending your time on important, high priority issues.

Part 1—Team Meetings

Why are Team Meetings so Important?

It is only through continued action that teams will deliver. The meetings are a place for the team to decide what the next actions should be, who should do them and by when. Obviously these decisions are in line with each team member's Role within The Plan, which is based on the Strategy, which leads to the Goals and Vision.

Communication within a team is essential to achieve a huge amount of team activities e.g. brainstorm creative ideas, agree on which ones they want to take forward, create a forum for helping each other find solutions to potholes/barriers, support each other emotionally so that everyone feels they can 'stay on the bus', deal with inevitable comparison and competition between team members, ensure that all members of the team are empowered to contribute fully, create a flexible team so that the vision/strategy/plan/roles can be changed if needed to ensure high delivery to the business, support each other when motivation is lacking or pick each other up after an inevitable knock (see Chapter 10).

What is a Successful Team Meeting?

High performing teams only have team meetings when they are needed for a business outcome. The purpose of the meetings will be:

- To make a group decision
- To brainstorm a solution to a problem
- To check that the work that the individual team members are doing is all aligned and to plan
- To share information about the external barriers to team delivery (see Chapter 9)
- To re-assess the vision, goals and plan in the light of an unforeseen event occurring

Developing High Delivery Teams

- To express held emotions if need be (although this is usually done in the pub after people have lost their inhibitions through alcohol!).

Of all my work in organisations, it's meetings that seem to be the most common way that teams under perform. There are often too many meetings, with no advanced agendas and no actual actions that those in the meetings agree to take. Or actions are agreed to but there is no follow up, and no repercussions if that person fails to complete their action.

Your Team Meeting Check

As a team manager, ask yourself

- Do my team enjoy these meetings, or have to be dragged there and feel they are a waste of time?
- Do I/they prioritise them over all other work?' If the answer to this is 'no' then the message is that your team is not managing its meetings effectively.
- Do we allocate an hour or two just out of habit?
- Do we have an agenda with written actions with deadlines and who is accountable from the last meeting?
- What happens if someone doesn't carry out the action that they committed to in a team meeting by the date they said they'd complete it?
- For other meetings in my organisation, do I know why I am meeting in advance, or do I just turn up because I've been invited?

When to Meet?

There is not a one size fits all when it comes to any of this work, but generally team meetings should be at the start of the day, so that nothing can get in the way. Ideally if they are weekly, have them on a Monday morning, so that psychologically the team leave the meeting knowing what their actions for the week are. At higher levels within organisations, team meetings move to fortnightly, monthly, quarterly (for some boards). So the team need to decide how often they feel they should meet and when.

High Performing Teams will have a mixture of meeting types:

One—The first type of meeting will be to set up the vision, SMART goals, strategy and plan and possibly the roles involved.

Two—Once the above has been agreed, the remaining meetings are to keep the bus on track and keep everyone in the bus! So these types of meetings will focus on questions that team members need resolving at a team level.

Three—Re-assessing where the team is against plan and budget is a third type of meeting which should be quick and efficient—reasons why the team is not on plan or budget should be discussed in meeting type 2, with the question 'what is stopping us from being on plan?' and 'is it possible to get back on plan?', 'what needs to happen for us to get back on plan?' or 'is it better to re-adjust the plan?'

The Agenda

For Executive Boards, draft agendas will be circulated weeks before the meeting and amended several times, for high delivery project teams, this will be an administrative burden. However a basic agenda is needed, even if you use the same structure for each meeting and simply change one or two agenda items.

- It is important that items on the agenda have a realistic estimated time against them, so that there is time to cover all items in the meeting.
- The Agenda should be circulated before the meeting so everyone knows what the purpose of the meeting is.
- There should be a chance for team members to contribute to the agenda, or at least raise things in the Any Other Business (AOB) section.

Developing High Delivery Teams

- It's also necessary to have agenda items phrased as an action, with a verb contained in the sentence e.g. *Discuss* xyz to *decide* what to do next, e.g. *Approve* increased budget for project y. e.g. *Understand* the new IT system and how it affects our processes, e.g. *Find* a solution to x problem and *agree* next action. If agenda items are simply listed 'discuss' then no action will be taken, if agenda items are listed as a noun 'New IT System' then its not clear what the purpose of the meeting is because all meetings need to end in action, even if its to swap information, or to decide not to do something!
- With problem solving in team meetings, its important for the team to agree if they have the power within the team to take the actions required to solve the problem/remove a barrier, or if they don't have the power. If they don't have the power to take the actions to solve the problem/remove the barrier, then they need to agree to escalate it to whoever does have the power in the organisation to take these actions.

The Essential Players

Chairperson—each meeting should have a chairperson (normally the team leader, but this can be rotated) whose responsibility it is, to keep the meeting on track and moving through the agenda. The chairperson also has the casting vote if the team need to vote to make a decision and there are equal numbers both sides.

Time Keeper—each meeting should have a time keeper (who is not the chairperson) whose role it is, to inform the team if they are running over the time allocated on the agenda for an item, this keeps the team focused and on track, often the team can decide to continue with the item in the Any Other Business section if there is time, or set it onto the next team meeting. Note: if agenda items keep being moved because no decision can be made, then that tells you that either the agenda item is not worded clearly and needs to be broken down into a series of questions, or that the group cannot make a decision because they need more information, or there is a problem with the group dynamic. Group dynamics is covered below.

Minute Taker—each meeting should have a minute taker (and this role should be rotated).

Effective Minute Taking

The minute taker need not record everything that is said, but simply list against the agenda items:

- The decisions that were made,
- The actions that were agreed to, by whom and the date by which it will be completed.
- The agenda items for next meeting and
- A section for any other comments e.g. if decisions were hard to make, if anyone wants their opinion about something recorded specifically, or if a guest was present and why.

Meetings Where Discussions Go Off Track

Some items on the agenda will raise questions amongst the team, a discussion will ensue and before you know it, you are out of time! The key is for someone (ideally the chairperson, but can be anyone) to notice that a discussion is going on and at that point to simply stop the discussion and ask

'What is the question here?'

This allows the team members to think about what they are discussing and verbalise the actual question(s) at the heart of the discussion. Once these questions are recorded then the discussion becomes a 'for' or 'against' decision and once everyone has had chance to air their views, the chairperson can call for a vote 'for or against' or 'option a, b or c?'.

Making Team Decisions—Unanimous Decision or Voting?

A common way for teams to under perform, is that the team only likes to make unanimous decisions.

If the whole team are not in agreement, then decisions never get made and arguments keep getting re-hashed meeting after meeting. The Team Leader getting the casting vote in the event of an even vote, means that teams can quickly make decisions and move on.

Note: it is important that anyone who cannot make the meeting, forfeits their right to vote on decisions required in that meeting. In some cases the majority of the team may decide that this decision is so important that it should be put on the next team meeting's agenda for full discussion, and to allow all team members to attend—or at least send in a proxy vote. (i.e. the team member who can't make the meeting, can let another member know how they would like to vote on the issues on the agenda and that can then be counted).

For highly contentious issues, it is advisable to have a Team Coach who can ensure that the group is 'held' in a safe place while difficult emotional reactions are processed by individuals in the team. If this does not happen, then unexpressed emotions can be trapped in the team and damage the team in the future, see Chapter 6.

Part 2—Group Dynamics

How Group Dynamics affect Team Discussion and Decision Making

Group dynamics loosely is the way in which a group interacts amongst itself. So who is the natural leader? How do the others group for safety or collaboration?

A team will have a natural group dynamic depending on the characters within it. This will obviously change each time a new member joins, or an old member leaves. The Leader of the team has the most powerful influence on the group dynamics and the unspoken rules of the behaviours that are allowed amongst the group and what behaviours are not (the true culture of the team).

Honest Open Communication

How a team makes decisions will be down to the group dynamics. High performing teams can make decisions based on the input of all team members, in the correct time frame. This is because each person in the team has a level of trust with the others so that they feel they can speak their truth on an issue and be heard and respected. (To have each member of a team act like this is actually quite unusual and often needs a bit of work because there are likely to be members who don't feel they can speak and be heard, so they either don't make any communication, or they make non-verbal communication).

Exercise 7—Making The Team Aware of The Group Dynamics

Note: A team leader can do this, but it is more likely that a qualified and experienced team coach who is an outsider to the organisation would do this exercise.

- During a team meeting, the leader or team coach observes the team discussing a topic on which they need to make a decision
- Having observed the communication flow (including non-verbal communication, such as people huffing, folding arms, sitting back, looking away etc . . .) the team coach can ask the team if they are ok to have it fed back to them by diagram?
- Assuming the team feel safe enough to be 'exposed' in this way, the team coach will whiteboard the flow of communication around the group. (The diagram will look like the mapping out of the movement of a pin ball in a pin ball machine because the communication bounces between the team members. The team coach can take a humorous gentle approach to allow their message to be best absorbed by the team).

- It is important to simply state what was observable without making any assumptions as to what the person was thinking or feeling. For example 'First Mark suggested that Ruth should project manage this and I saw that you, Anne moved back a little and looked down, I wondered if you were keen to project manage and were disappointed? . . . then Ruth you looked at Anne and then back at Mark without replying, perhaps you noticed Anne's response too?' As the team coach gently draws out the diagram of what they observed, they can make suggestions, or ask questions (in a very gentle way) of each participant, but never state that they know what is going on (because in fact, they don't and could be absolutely wrong!). This needs to be done sympathetically and in an enquiring way, where each person has a chance to first recognise how they reacted, and either accept it and discuss it, or perhaps chose to deny it. (If it is denied, then the coach mustn't press the point as the coach may have made a mistake or the person is still unaware of their unconscious communication signals or is not ready to openly discuss their reactions. If the latter is the case then they are still likely to reflect on it and talk about it when/if they are ready to, sometimes in a totally confidential one to one session at a later date with the team coach).

Note: There are innumerable types of communication diagrams that the team coach may observe, it is the skill of the coach to pick the pattern. It is also the experience of the coach that allows them to remain calm and centred throughout this exercise, even though some team members may have emotional reactions to what is being said. Compassion, respect and humour are often required from the team coach in these delicate exercises.

How This Exercise Works

The exercise works by the team coach using their own body as a feedback system, they are also part of the system, so if they see/hear a communication, they will automatically make a meaning from it because they are also human and have been conditioned by the same world where we are always trying to make sense of communications. (Different cultures may need a coach from their own culture to interpret these communications and feed them back to the group) The team coach is sitting in every person's shoes for an instant to imagine what might be going on for that person based on what they see/hear. It is the team coach that then has the courage to state what they thought might be going on for each person and why (their observable evidence). They must always be respectful of the fact that they have 'made up' what they think is actually going on in their own heads, so they need to check this out with each person they are addressing.

The purpose of this exercise is to get the team to express 'what is not being said'. This builds more open and honest communication in teams, and a more robust team for heated discussions and hugely varied opinions. The team coach is only looking to expose communication patterns that lead to a loss of performance e.g. Where a team communicates in such a way that decisions are made by just two people and the others don't contribute, or when a team cannot agree on anything because of the group dynamic.

Chapter 8—Team Relationships

There are relational dynamics within a team. Each person in the team has a relationship with all of the others. Therefore in a team of 4 people called John, Sue, Anne and Charles, there will be 6 different relationships playing out;

John and Sue
John and Anne
John and Charles
Sue and Anne
Sue and Charles
Anne and Charles

There may also be a secondary dynamic of John and Sue verses Anne and Charles etc . . . so the diagram becomes even more complex with larger teams. The relationships will also be influenced by seniority so if John is the Leader of the team, he will naturally have a different relationships with Sue, Anne and Charles.

Valuing Difference

Ultimately we are all different so good teams are made up of people who see the world in different ways, all feel they can express their point of view and that each member is valued for their differences.

Often Team Building exercises start with the team completing a psychological profile each and then discussing each other's differences. This is a good starting ground for appreciating that not everyone thinks, feels and sees the world the same way. These tools are useful only if the team then understand how they can change to improve their inter-team relationships and work better together in the future.

We are often made to feel that we should always be 'positive' at work otherwise we will bring the morale of the team down. However life is full of potholes and as we start to plan our journey towards our team goals, there is often a very useful person in the team whose mind is configured to imagining all the things that could go wrong on the journey—they see all the potential potholes. This person, the critic, is often put down, or dismissed as 'negative' but I always champion this person's input because difference in teams make them stronger. This person is the risk assessor, the person who can pre-empt what might go wrong so that the rest of the team can start to devise strategies for minimizing the risks.

Why Are Good Team Relationships Important?

In a high performing team, there are key traits such as trust, respect and open honest communication between the team members. These traits are the basis for good relationships anywhere, however within a team, there may be a couple of people who for some reason do not have as good a relationship as they could. This will prevent the team from openly discussing issues, making good decisions and keeping everyone in the team bus.

How we have Good and Bad Relationships

We tend to think that people can't read our thoughts, and of course they can't literally read our minds, but they pick up the 'vibe' of how we feel towards them, and the more emotionally intelligent they are, the more likely they are to pick this up and get it almost right!

This is a scary thought, because we are actually quite transparent and if we don't like someone they and other observers will probably know. They may not realise why, but they will probably not feel comfortable in your presence and therefore stay away from you—or if they can't do that, because they are in your team, they will move into a 'flight' or 'fight' mode (they will be anxious and therefore try to ignore you, no eye contact and very basic communication, or be actively angry with you and criticise you, or be passively aggressive by deliberately ignoring you to undermine you, or roll their eyes, shake their head to indicate their lack of respect/agreement etc . . .).If you see behaviours like this in a team, you know that there are relational problems that are holding the team back.

How To Improve Team Relationships

The good news is that when we are in relationship with someone we are in a system that has feedback, so when one person does or says something, the other person reacts, and then the first person reacts to this and so on. This is the process of either falling in love (when the interactions are mostly positive) or getting into a fight (when the interactions are mostly negative).

So to improve a relationship it's important to know what we are thinking about that person. They are much more than just the box we have put them in, and if it's a work relationship we don't get to see how they are with their families, or understand their history and childhood struggles that may have led them to behave in ways that irritate or upset us.

First we must understand that what we tend to focus on about someone is the key to how we feel about them. Then open our minds to considering that we don't know everything about them, and we don't understand why they are how they are. It's important to also have a general belief, that no—one is born evil, that we are all just struggling to get along in life the best way we know how! (Some of us have got better strategies for getting on with others that's true, we may have had better models as children and therefore have a head start which we should be grateful for, not take a superior attitude to those who didn't have this luxury). It's also important to understand that this person may, deep down, have their own insecurities (as we all do in life) about who they are, what they've done and if anyone will like them.

Once we can focus on anything that may be positive or understanding about them for example:

> They are hardworking and intelligent,
> They do have other friends,
> They may be lonely,
> They may feel concerned about their role in the organisation,
> They have huge pressures at work that they are struggling to cope with,

Then our feelings towards them change too and we are more open to building a better relationship with them. They will unconsciously feel a change when they are interacting with us too (even if this is only on the phone and not face to face) and eventually they may feel less judged and more accepted and therefore warm towards us.

Getting in our own way

Often we just want to be 'right' and therefore it is hard for us to change, the ego doesn't want to give up its position, which says I'm 'right' but the rest of the world should change! This is ok but it's also a way of staying stuck. If what you really want is to reach a goal, it could be this attitude and refusal to change that is getting in your way. Even though it's not easy, it is much easier to change ourselves than to change others, or change the world around us. Sometimes we need to adjust the goal to ensure that the achievement of the goal is entirely in our control—as opposed to a goal that is reliant on others e.g. my goal is to be promoted by September . . . It is better to re-phrase the goal to 'my goal is to find 3 potential roles that would represent a promotion, ask the decision makers what I need to do to get these roles and where possible do that'.

Your Boss is Not Your Parent

It is quite common for people to transfer a relationship they had with a parent or highly influential person in their childhood onto a relationship with their manager (or a stakeholder who is more senior to them).

This means that if they had a highly critical, domineering father, they may have learned to stay quiet and obey as a child. When they meet their new boss, if this new boss is male and criticises them or appears to be telling them what to do, they will automatically react as they did as a child, which will be to stay quiet and obey.

They will also start to feel towards this new boss as they felt towards their father and their level of emotion (fear, anger, guilt etc . . .) may be much higher than is rationally expected from the interactions that take place between them and their boss. The same pattern can obviously be transferred from a child/mother relationship to a female boss who may, in the eyes of the team member, have traits similar to their mother.

As a Team Coach, if someone is having a relationship problem with anyone who they perceive to be more senior, more experienced, or (in any way in a more powerful, parent like role to them), then I ask if that person reminds them in any way of one of their parents, or someone who was older than them from their past. Often this highlights that transference is occurring and once that person is aware of it, they can separate out their boss from their parent and deal with them as an adult.

Personality Traits

In theory, we have the capacity to have all personality traits and we are socialised to develop others more than some, those traits that are acceptable to our parents (or whoever cared for us in childhood) become those we demonstrate most, the negative traits we can admit to are those that are not ideal but still acceptable and those that we deny and fear are those that are unacceptable (either in society, or unacceptable from our parents/caregivers).

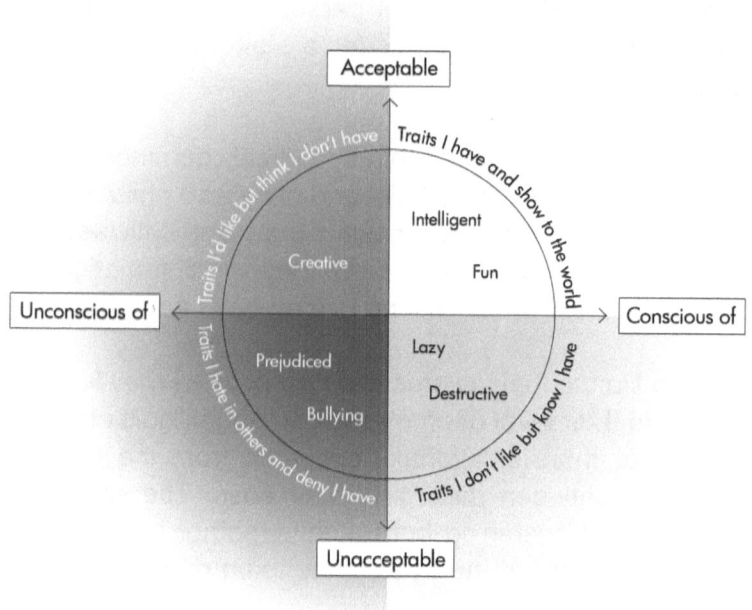

So if we have a personality trait that we really can't bear in ourselves, (or can't even acknowledge that we could ever have this trait) and project it onto others e.g. We can't bear selfishness and we often see others behaving selfishly.

At work we will not only see lots of behaviour from others that we interpret as 'selfish' but we also then find it hard to have a good relationship with that person. Other colleagues at work could be often moaning about their job/boss/colleague but we are happy to be friends with them, so long as they don't show any traits of selfishness!

Exercise 7: Building Good Team Relationships

- This whole exercise needs to be confidential, so that each person works on their own and does not have to report any of their answers to the questions below if they do not want to. The exercise is to demonstrate how we have good relationships and also to hopefully move each team member to improve a relationship with another team member if it is not already good.
- Ask the team as a whole to think of the person they like best at work.
- Then to write this person's name down in their own note books.
- Then ask them to describe this person in a few words and write that down too.
- Next to write down how they feel when they think of having a meeting with this person.
- Next they need to pick a person who they do not have a good relationship with at work.
- Write down a description of this person in a few words too.
- Next write down how they feel when they think of having a meeting with this person. (Some humour may be needed here as feelings will show on faces and little exasperated sounds may be made, as a Coach, it's always good to let each person in the team know that what they feel is OK and that they are not being judged)
- A general discussion about the difference can be had at this point, and the explanation above regarding How We Have Good or Bad Relationships.
- The next phase of this exercise, is to get each team member to close their eyes and breathe deeply (this is to relax them, so that they are in a resourceful and open space)
- Then to imagine that they are in the shoes of the person they do not have a good relationship with. To imagine what that person must be feeling when they behave is certain ways, to write this down.
- Then to ask yourself 'what could this person's experience in life have led them to believe about themselves, others, the

world? Write this down too. (We often carry generic ideas about ourselves, others and the world, for example, 'I'm not good with people', 'whatever I do I'm not good enough', 'the world is dangerous, we must always be looking out for what could go wrong'.
- As the coach it's time to check in to see if anyone has had any shift in feeling towards this person—some may feel sorry for them, others may realise that their own approach is making this person feel worse, some may not have a shift because their ego still wants to be 'right' and this person be 'wrong'.
- Finally as a team you can end with asking them to write down what they think of their other team members (again just confidentially in their own note books and there will be no need to share this—unless it is all positive!). This exercise will already allow them to know who they'd like to build a better relationship with and how. Its important not to overplay doing this right here and now in the room with the team, because often with change work like this, people want to take more control and decide when and where they will re-do this exercise for anyone of their team mates.

Chapter 9—External Barriers

Road Rage!

As your team bus happily cruises down the road towards the team goals, there are other buses, cars and bikes on the road that could cause your team no end of road rage!

These other drivers are within your organisation and to some extent the risks of them not delivering and therefore preventing your team from delivering on time can be minimized.

To do this the team needs to look at where the team fits into the whole organisation and which other teams interface with your team. As your team is unlikely to be an independent island, but part of a bigger more complex system, you need to start working with others beyond yourselves.

Some organisations will need to react quickly to changing market needs/trends and therefore any long term planning for your team will often be derailed. It is better in these cultures to find the optimum length goal (say 3 or 6 months) and focus on these. In other organisations it's possible to plan for much longer with the knowledge that the leaders are unlikely to derail these plans.

The Wider Implications of Team Coaching

If a team within a bigger system actively improves its ability to deliver, then it will raise the game of the teams around it—eventually, like ripples on a pond, the rest of the organisation will benefit, from just one team improving. So by improving the performance of your team you are creating organisational level development.

Team Test for External Barriers

- What are the critical things that your team needs to rely on others for?

- Have you got a history of other teams/people in the organisation not doing their part correctly and affecting the delivery of your team?
- If all other teams worked effectively what would this mean for your team?
- What happens if there are other influences on your team that stop members getting to work/being able to work?
- Do you have any cross-skilling programmes so team members can cover each other's roles?

As a team you may need to call an 'Emergency Meeting' to tackle a major problem that is lying in your way. High performing teams will be able to all work together to brainstorm ways around the barrier. If the team bus finds a fallen tree in the road, the bus must stop for a moment while the team get out and work out the best way to get round, or remove the barrier.

- How quickly do you know as a team that there is a barrier in your path?
- Do you need to nominate a scout, or have a process that gives you early warning signs of problems ahead?

Exercise 8: Minimising Impact of External Barriers

- As a team place a circle in the middle of a whiteboard or flip chart and add the name of your team in this circle.
- Brainstorm all the other teams/people that your team has to interact with and place them around your team circle in their own circles.
- Look at the interfaces and decide which ones are critical to the performance of your team—star these in red.
- Of these interfaces ask yourselves 'which of these critical interfaces do I need to actively manage to help them to perform their part in the system to ensure our team can deliver well?'
- Start to brainstorm ways in which your team can manage these other teams/people to ensure they don't derail your team. Have an actual plan with the names of who in the

team will be responsible for what with regard to this. (e.g. John will contact the ops team 2 weeks before the go live date to ensure they are on time with their work too).
- Next, the team needs to brainstorm other things that could go wrong that are out of their control e.g. Train strikes on critical days so key members can't get to work. This is where the critic in the team will be really valuable.
- Only take the risks that will most affect the team delivery and are most likely to happen. (This is not an exercise on what to do if the whole company or whole of your city/country was affected. Only choose the sensible, obvious things that could derail your team's delivery)
- Discuss a plan of action to minimize these risks, e.g. John and Jane will cross skill, so if one of them is ill, or cannot make it to work on the critical days, the other knows what to do on their behalf.

Chapter 10—The Leader

The Quality of the Bus Driver

As a leader of a team you will automatically be the 'model' of acceptable team behaviour. So if you come in late each day, or get angry with a certain area of the business, then your team will follow suit and unconsciously begin to do the same.

- How good are you a steering the bus straight in a storm?
- Can you keep everyone in the bus calm and focused on their roles when the bus is careering all over the road trying to avoid the potholes?
- Do you feel happy and motivated in your job, or are you going into work carrying low performance energy?

The Leader's Influence on Team Culture

What is Culture? A group of people is like a living system, that has rules of behaviour that are sometime conscious to the team members e.g. As a team we don't tolerate shouting at each other, or unconscious e.g. As a team its acceptable to be late for a team meeting but not acceptable to go home before 6.30pm on a Monday night.

These rules will not have been spoken about, but will have just been picked up as common behaviours and new team members will soon begin copying the others behaviours, so a dynamic is present. The Leader has the biggest influence on creating these rules and acceptable behaviours and subsequently has the greatest power to change the team culture to one of high performance. The way in which they act, what they accept and do not accept from others, what they personally like and dislike etc. influence the behaviours and attitudes of those they lead.

Developing High Delivery Teams

It is not necessary for a team to know consciously all their rules of behaviour. It is only necessary to unearth them if they are preventing the team from performing to their best and delivering their goals.

You are the Model of Behaviour and Attitudes

Although there is still a debate amongst neurophysiologists, they have discovered specific neurons in the brain that have been called 'mirror neurons'. They believe these neurons are there to help us mirror or copy the behaviour of those around us. This is how, as children, we learn to speak with the same accent as our family, we learn to walk and then learn all of the socially acceptable and non-acceptable behaviours that our culture holds. We don't need to be told these things; we just start to copy the adults we spend a lot of time with.

This same phenomenon is occurring in the workplace and this is how we form cultures. The behaviours and attitudes of the leader of a group of people will be mirrored by those around him or her. Groups of people also mirror each other and eventually a culture of unspoken, unconscious behavioural norms form. It's only when a person does something that is not the cultural norm that anyone notices.

- What are your thoughts about other areas of your organisation/other teams/other people?
- How do you behave towards other people within your organisation?
- Who do you get frustrated with?
- Who makes you feel uncomfortable, who do you avoid and why?

Many books have been written on Leadership and this is not the forum, but the quality of a team is most influenced by the quality of their leader. You may have inherited a team that you would not have recruited, but a good leader will be able to either fairly and honestly performance manage out those who cannot perform, or coach the team to raise their levels of performance and the way they interact with each other.

Appreciating Each Team Member Equally

It is natural for us to gravitate to those most like us—that is how organisations can recruit similar people and end up with a strong culture, but one that is not very adaptable to a changing outside environment. So as a leader if you find it easier to appreciate some team members over others, look at the ones that you are struggling to connect with. What is different about them to you, without judgement, notice how they contribute something else to the team that perhaps you could not. Leaders of High Performing Teams will appreciate each team member equally despite their differences.

Creating Adult to Adult relationships rather than Parent to Child

- As a leader are you often frustrated that your team don't take responsibility?
- Are you tired with always having to think for them, and innovate?
- Would you like them to 'step up to the mark' and take more ownership?

I'm often asked to coach a team where the leader is facing the above problems. They want me to change the members of the team, but don't realise that they are also part of the problem.

There is a direct relationship between how the team behave (i.e. not taking responsibility, coming up with ideas and taking ownership) and how the leader behaves.

How is this common problem created?

Often in hierarchical structures where there is a manager above you and people below you that report to you, we develop a leadership style that is more like parenting. Because our first model of leadership is from our own parents and as we psychologically grow into adults we develop our own internal parent part (so that we don't need parents any more and can live and survive in the world with our own internal parental part guiding us).

Do you have this problem?

If you are more like a parent as a leader, then you will be looking at your team members as if they are more like children that need you to help them, look after them, or tell them off when they are naughty! If as a leader you have been acting more like a parent then the team will automatically be acting more like children—that is the theory. So you will have helped to create a team with these types of problems;

- you will not trust your team to work unsupervised,
- you will feel that they cannot resolve conflict between themselves so
- you need to step in and sort out relationship problems,
- you will be the sole driver of the direction and ideas and
- they will wait for you to tell them what to do.

How to resolve it?

Does this sound familiar? Then how you make changes, is by first changing yourself. They key is for you to act more like an equal adult, and less like a parent towards them. (Think of how you behave in relationship to your friends that you respect as equal adults).

If you are more like an equal adult type leader, then you will view your team as equal adults who have full capability, don't need protecting, or supervising. By holding this view and by trusting that your team are all equally capable adults, you will act differently towards them. They in turn will gradually start to act less like children and more like the equal, capable adults that they are.

This will lead to them taking responsibility, ownership and coming up with their own ideas. Because they actually are all adults, this change (although potentially scary to start with) will be much more empowering for them and their future careers.

Note: This is the same process parents need to go through with teenage children who are actually growing into adults and at the same time need to feel that their parent trusts and respects them as equal capable adults.

Case Study

I was asked to coach a team where the team leader had been promoted from the head of the UK team to head of Europe. This meant that he didn't have as much time as he had in the past to spend with the UK team. He was travelling to meet his other teams across Europe.

Those in the UK team were worried that they had lost their leader and would not be able to function so well.

The majority of the coaching work was to enable the UK team to shift from behaving like children all vying for the attention and good favour of their 'dad' to feeling more like equal, capable adults who could work collaboratively without the need to bring in the leader to resolve conflicts, make decisions or set team goals and timeframes. I also needed to work with the leader to ensure that he started to feel and act towards the members of the UK team differently. In the past he would have stepped in to resolve disagreements and been the ultimate decision maker for the team. Now he needed to trust that his team would be able to have heated debates, but then come to a team decision about the best way forward and that each member of the team would honour that decision and work collaboratively, even if they had been outvoted at the team meeting.

In this case the changes need to be made by everyone in the team, the team members had to 'grow up' and feel more empowered and the team leader had to become more like an equal adult, and less like a parent when dealing with his team members.

Exercise 10: Raising Team Awareness

Part 1—to be conducted by the Leader alone (normally in a 1:1 Coaching session)

- Write down what you think about each team member—do it quickly, instinctively and honestly as this will not be seen by anyone else. You only need a few lines about each one, as if you were describing them to a good friend who doesn't work in your organisation.
- Have a look at your answers and see which team members you are holding 'negative' thoughts about. They will sense this to some extent. This is the area of development as a Leader you need to work on. Assuming you are 'stuck' with the team you currently have (most of us are!) then for each person you have 'negative thoughts' about, try and write down some more positive ones. They must be true, they can include empathy thoughts eg 'they struggle with xyz', 'they need to feel more secure to reach their potential'
- Read these positive statements about each team member every morning on the way to work and regularly throughout the day. This is consciously choosing to change how you relate to these team members and therefore change how they begin to feel about themselves/you/work and therefore change how they then begin to act. (Trust that if you do this diligently and sincerely, they will act more positively, eventually contributing more to the success of the team, or have the confidence to at least deal with a key issue, or own up to feeling that they need some help etc.) You can't change someone else without changing your own way of relating to them first.
- Write down what you think your team would say to the following questions about you: What area of the job does he/she enjoy doing most? What area does he/she least enjoy? Does he/she have a favoured team member, if so who is it and why? Does he/she have a least favoured team member if so who is it and why? Does he/she like their job?

- Look at your answers and assess if there are any changes in attitude you need to make, so that you are really seen in the light you wish to be. (This is easier said than done, and may include a Leader working with a Coach and using a Leadership Profiling Tool to unearth the key areas for development.)

Part 2—to be conducted by the Team anonymously (normally in a Team Coaching session when the Leader is deliberately not present)

- What does your leader do that most annoys you?
- What does your leader do that you appreciate most?
- If you were to be totally honest, what would you say about your leader? (Answer this quickly and instinctively, just a few lines off the top of your head).
- Can you have open, honest conversations about your work, how you feel about it and your difficulties with your leader?
- Do you think your leader knows what you're good at and will help you develop in your career?
- Once the answers are collated anonymously, then can be fed back (sympathetically by the Team Coach) to the Leader, to help the Leader identify areas that they'd like to work on.
- One more step can be to ask each team member, what they think their team members and team Leader would say about them? Things they do well and things they could do better? This also ensures that each team member, has to do some self-analysis and take responsibility for their own input into the team. (Often teams can simply blame their Leader or the Organisation which means they have already given away their power to change things for the better. Once members of a team realise that they are all equal parts of the system and therefore all equally contribute to the morale and output of the team, they can start to identify what they'd like to do/think that's different to their normal way of working).

Chapter 11—Managing Energy

Stopping For Petrol

Everything in nature follows a sin curve. We have summer followed by winter, day followed by night, birth followed by death. So why is it that at work we expect ourselves to be able to work at 100% energy permanently? This is not only unnatural but unsustainable in the medium to long term.

When working with teams I encourage them to place the key times when the team will need to work at 100% along their plan. Then to ensure that following these peak performances, the team builds into their plan some down time.

This does not need to mean that they do no work at all, but perhaps this is the time to take holiday, or work more regular hours. Over time the deliverable can creep up as the team become more efficient. They can do more in the time available. Rather than just all working longer hours.

But This Is Unrealistic For My Organisation.

This may seem unlikely for many organisations, however once the team has clear vision, SMART goals and a plan where everyone is doing the role that they are best suited to, then teams have built in the capability to deliver what is expected of them (and more) and still have time to recover.

High performing sports teams will follow this rule by gearing up for their matches, but also ensure that their team players rest and recover following peak performance times.

For teams that are reactive by nature (e.g. emergency services) this may not be possible. However many teams that do not need to work in such a reactive way are stuck in a reactive mode because they haven't yet taken the time to step back see the bigger picture and think strategically. They have not yet taken control of their own time and energy. This is obviously harder to achieve for teams embedded in reactive cultures, but not impossible. The best organisations are ones where the top team (Board Level) invest in the time to be high performing and strategic rather than reactive and political.

Thoughts Create Reality

Listen to the statements that you and your team make about the state of the organization and the state of the market that it's operating in. Write down verbatim some of the sentences that are spoken by team member, so you can show them exactly what thoughts they are holding in their heads (we often run the same thought over and over again without hearing it, like a mantra).

- Are the statements negative or positive?
- Do you and your team realize that this is what you are running over and over like a tape recording in your heads?
- When you think these thoughts/statements how does it effect your energy?
- Do you notice that the negative thoughts create a loss of energy? Or a gain of frustrated energy?
- Which thoughts are useful i.e. have good information in them, and which are simply fear based with nothing you can do about them?

From an energy perspective, its useful to hear our thoughts, some are fear based and carry very good warnings about what could happen in the future if we don't do something today—these are the ones to listen carefully to and ask 'so what could I do to allay this fear right now?' Then act on this.

Some of the thoughts will create an angry/frustrated energy and again, its important to listen to these and ask 'so what is this telling me I need to do/not do right now?' Then act on this.

Some of the thoughts will be purely negative about the economy, the market, the organization, the team, myself . . . if you have asked

Developing High Delivery Teams

'is there anything I can/need to do regarding this thought?' and the answer is 'NO' then you need to swap these thoughts for some more energy conserving ones e.g

- 'Actually no-one knows what will happen with the economy, and I'm sure I'll survive whatever does happen.'
- 'We can't control other people, but I can decide how to react to them and I chose to just focus on me and let them get on with it'
- 'In times of great change, there are great opportunities, if we stay calm and keep an open mind we will find them'
- 'What is good about this organization, this market we're in, this team I lead?'

Many leaders that I have coached through tough times have felt at one stage that they or their companies are in survival mode. If the leaders of businesses continue to view it in this way, then through their fear, they will generate this as a reality. Clients and future employees in the market place will pick up this 'desperation' and this is not the buzz that successful companies create.

Positive Thoughts and Energy Lead to Expansion

Organisations that flourish and grow despite difficult times are those that have people running them that are holding positive thoughts and therefore positive energy, the teams within these organisations are energized and feeling relatively happy and safe, so they act from this base—trying new things, seeing opportunites where others don't, being pleasant to work with and attracting top talent and also more clients.

Negative Thoughts and Energy Lead to Contraction

Organisations that have leaders holding negative thoughts and therefore fear-based energy will feel that they need to stay safe. They will not make big risky decisions that could lead to expansion, they will act to conserve what they have, all the while fearing that what they have will diminish. Ironically this energy base for a company has no other logical outcome but for failure to adapt and survive.

Specific conscious work is required at a team level to decide how the leaders want to represent their company in their own minds, therefore how they will feel about their company, their own careers, their security and also the emotional state from which they act each day.

Case Study

I was brought in to work with a team that had lost 3 people in the previous 2 months. One of the 3 had been given 6 weeks off for stress. The organisation was blaming the team leader. However when I first met the team I realised that they were all exhausted. They actually enjoyed what they did and the leader was incredibly diligent. The team had just completed a major deal and were still expected to work on the next one immediately.

They had no concept in the organisation of rest and recovery. The expectation in their culture was to work at maximum energy, 100% of the time and employees were regularly doing 90 hour weeks!

Needless to say, despite very high salaries the staff turnover across the whole company was high. The cost of replacing people and covering sick leave was enormous and could easily be prevented. The board would not be persuaded and eventually the leader of the team left the organisation too. The productivity of the team was high but totally unsustainable and unfortunately the skill set and business knowledge in the team walked away.

Exercise 11: Optimising Team Energy—Being Sustainable

- As a team take your plan and decide what key activities are going to occur in the future
- Plot these along the time line as Milestones
- Then decide how long you need as a recovery period following these key milestones

- Pilot these periods along the timeline and brainstorm what things would lead the team to compromising their recovery period and not keeping the boundaries around this time period strong.
- Add these possible risks into the plan too

Chapter 12—Celebrating Success

Why Is Celebrating So Important?

It Builds Employer-Employee Relationship—Loyalty

If team members have worked really hard and delivered a key part of the plan, then they deserve to have recognition as well as something that they value from their employer.

Employer-employee relationships are like any other type of relationship, in that both parties need to give and take. Many people feel that their employer doesn't care about them at all, just takes as much of their time and energy that they can and gives nothing but the salary in return.

This is how employers end up with no employee loyalty and a merry go round of employees who will readily leave for a higher salary with a competitor.

Organisations Don't Need to Offer Even Higher Salaries

Often companies believe that if they pay their staff more money and bonuses, then they will work harder and be loyal to the company.

In my experience money doesn't buy people into their company (particularly at more senior levels when people have matured and recognised that their salary is not the be all and end all).

In reality we like to feel valued for our contribution not through a standard annual salary, but by being told by your manager or senior stakeholders that they appreciate all your hard work.

- As a leader when was the last time you congratulated a team member on a piece of work?
- Do you know what keeps each of your team members motivated?

- How do your team like to celebrate?
- Would you work for a company that paid slightly less if you felt valued, part of a high performing team and had fun at work?

Maintaining Motivation

We are all different with regard to how we stay motivated. Some people can work towards a 5 year goal and some need 3 month goals in order to stay focused.

To enable teams to maintain high energy throughout a longer project, it's vital to celebrate delivering key components. These should be marked as Key Milestones on the project plan.

Breaking down a larger goal into smaller components and celebrating each one, allows those in the team that could be overwhelmed by the enormity of a longer term goal, to focus on each phase of the plan separately.

How to Celebrate?

Often teams are 'forced' to do team activities like going bowling, or playing team games, however some people feel uncomfortable with this and resentful that it is taking up more of their personal time.

There are things that leaders can offer their teams that cost nothing e.g. a chance to have a morning off in lieu of working all weekend, or paying for a team lunch in the local pub. Even leaving at 3pm on a Friday to go for team drinks (assuming that everyone in the team is happy with the pub environment) can cost nothing and take nothing away from the productivity of the company.

Acknowledgments

I would like to acknowledge all of the teams that I've worked with over the years and particularly the leaders who have had the foresight and courage to bring me into their organisation and trust me to help raise the team to the highest level.

I'd also like to acknowledge my own team who have helped me enormously with proof reading, sense checking and always encouraging me to 'just get on with it and finish the book'! Thank you.

For more tips and information on how to create high performing Leaders, Teams and Organisations please contact Rebecca Watson at Brompton Associates.

www.bromptonassociates.com

www.ingramcontent.com/pod-product-compliance
Lightning Source LLC
Chambersburg PA
CBHW021015180526
45163CB00005B/1966